SOCIAL SECURITY LEGISLATION 2015/16

VOLUME II:
INCOME SUPPORT, JOBSEEKER'S ALLOWANCE, STATE PENSION CREDIT AND THE SOCIAL FUND

SOCIAL SECURITY LEGISLATION 2015/16

General Editor
Nick Wikeley, M.A. (Cantab)

VOLUME II:
INCOME SUPPORT, JOBSEEKER'S ALLOWANCE, STATE PENSION CREDIT AND THE SOCIAL FUND

Commentary By

Penny Wood, LL.B., M.Sc.
District Tribunal Judge

Richard Poynter, B.C.L., M.A. (Oxon.)
District Tribunal Judge,
Judge of the Upper Tribunal

Nick Wikeley, M.A. (Cantab)
Temporary Chamber President, War Pensions and Armed Forces Compensation
Chamber, Judge of the Upper Tribunal, Emeritus Professor of Law,
University of Southampton

John Mesher, B.A., B.C.L. (Oxon), LL.M. (Yale)

Consultant Editor
Child Poverty Action Group

SWEET & MAXWELL   THOMSON REUTERS

Published in 2015 by Thomson Reuters (Professional) UK Limited
trading as Sweet & Maxwell, Friars House,
160 Blackfriars Road, London, SE1 8EZ.
(Registered in England and Wales. Company No 1679046.
Registered office: 2nd Floor, 1 Mark Square, Leonard Street,
London EC2A 4EG)

For further information on our products and services, visit
http://www.sweetandmaxwell.co.uk

Typeset by Servis Filmsetting Ltd, Stockport, Cheshire
Printed and bound by CPI Group (UK) Ltd, Croydon, CR0 4YY

ISBN 978-0-414-03905-6

No natural forests were destroyed to make this product;
only farmed timber was used and replanted.

A CIP catalogue record for this book is available
from the British Library

CHILD POVERTY ACTION GROUP

The Child Poverty Action Group (CPAG) is a charity, founded in 1965, which campaigns for the relief of poverty in the United Kingdom. It has a particular reputation in the field of welfare benefits law derived from its legal work, publications, training and parliamentary and policy work, and is widely recognised as the leading organisation for taking test cases on social security law.

CPAG is therefore ideally placed to act as Consultant Editor to this 5-volume work—**Social Security Legislation 2015/16**. CPAG is not responsible for the detail of what is contained in each volume, and the authors' views are not necessarily those of CPAG. The Consultant Editor's role is to act in an advisory capacity on the overall structure, focus and direction of the work.

For more information about CPAG, its rights and policy publications or training courses, its address is 30 Micawber Street, London, N1 7TB (telephone: 020 7837 7979—website: *http://www.cpag.org.uk*).

FOREWORD

Changes in substantive law rarely lead to simplicity, often layer upon layer of complexity is added to deal with the unexpected and unintended consequences of earlier legislation. In a rapidly changing world further complexity is added because of a need to deal with the quickening pace of change. What is needed then is an authoritative guide allowing for both necessary detail and yet a clear and concise explanation. Hence the great value placed upon this series, an invaluable guide to legislation in this field. I and the Tribunal as a whole are greatly indebted to those who have contributed to these indispensable volumes and thus rendered such assistance to our work.

Judge John Aitken
President
Social Entitlement Chamber
First-tier Tribunal

PREFACE

Income Support, Jobseeker's Allowance, State Pension Credit and the Social Fund is Volume II of what is now a five-volume series: *Social Security Legislation 2015/16*. The companion volumes are: Bonner, Hooker, Poynter, White, Wikeley and Wood, *Volume I: Non-Means Tested Benefits and Employment and Support Allowance;* Rowland and White, *Volume III: Administration, Adjudication and the European Dimension;* Wikeley, Williams and Hooker, *Volume IV: Tax Credits and HMRC-administered Social Security Benefits*; and Mesher, Poynter, Wikeley and Wood, *Volume V: Universal Credit.*

Each of the volumes in the series provides a legislative text, clearly showing the form and date of amendments, and commentary up to date to April 13, 2015. The commentary in this volume includes case law developments up to the end of July 2015.

This book goes to press as welfare reform continues to play a central role in domestic politics. In pursuit of its aim to reduce welfare spending by £12 billion, the Government has published its Welfare Reform and Work Bill 2015/2016. Headlines include the reduction of the benefit cap to £23,000 per year (£15,410 for single people) in Greater London and £20,000 per year (£13,400 for single people) elsewhere; the freezing of certain benefits and tax credits for four years from April 2016; limiting the number of children that can be included in child tax credit and universal credit awards to two, removal of the work-related activity component in ESA and the limited capability for work element in universal credit; and help with mortgage interest to be by way of interest-bearing loans secured on claimants' homes. In addition, many other smaller cutbacks are to be introduced, in particular in relation to the calculation of entitlement to tax credits and universal credit. These are of course in addition to the changes introduced by the previous coalition government, for example, the restrictions on entitlement of EEA jobseekers to benefit (see the commentary to reg.21AA of the Income Support Regulations in this volume for analysis of these changes).

At the same time, the roll-out of universal credit is slowly gathering some momentum—it is intended that new claims will finally be extended to the whole of the country by the end of April 2016 but only for a restricted category of claimant. In most areas this continues to be single claimants without responsibility for children who meet the gateway conditions, although claims from those with children can now be made in the first 27 "relevant districts" in which universal credit has been introduced. Extending the coverage of universal credit beyond this restricted, "straightforward" category of claimant to, for example those with low earnings from self-employment, presents a formidable challenge, not only for the Government but also for the claimants who are affected. The cost also continues to rise—according to the Major Projects Authority's annual report published on June 25, 2015, the whole life cost of implementing universal credit is now estimated at £15.85 billion (an increase of £3 billion since the 2012 estimate).

Meanwhile, the primary focus of the main legislative changes during the last year, as far as the benefits covered by this volume are concerned, has been on (i) JSA, and (ii) the "right to reside" test. This is perhaps unsurprising, given the Government's emphasis on getting people into work and its concern about the lure of the UK's benefits system for migrants.

In terms of caselaw, the developments in relation to sanctions, in particular those imposed in connection with a "failure" under a scheme under s.17A of the Jobseekers Act 1995 ("Work for your benefit" schemes) continue. The decision of the Upper Tribunal three-judge panel (*SSWP v TJ (JSA)* [2015] UKUT 56 (AAC)) convened to determine issues left outstanding by the *Reilly and Wilson* and *Reilly (No.2)* litigation and was issued on February 11, 2015. The Upper Tribunal identified seven issues that arose in the cases before it. However, the position remains unresolved as the Upper Tribunal immediately granted the Secretary of State permission to appeal to the Court of Appeal on two of the issues, namely the extent of the retrospective effect of the Jobseekers (Back to Work Schemes) Act 2013 on ordinary canons of statutory construction, and if the decision was wrong on that, the proper construction of the Act as required by s.3 of the Human Rights Act 1998. The appeal is currently listed for hearing in November 2015, on the same date as that in *Reilly (No.2)* (which is the Secretary of State's appeal against the High Court's decision that the purported retrospective validation of the JSA (Employment, Skills and Enterprise Scheme) Regulations 2011 by the 2013 Act breached the claimants' right to a fair trial under art.6 ECHR). Another of the issues dealt with by the Upper Tribunal was whether there was a lack of sufficient prior information such that the requirement to participate in the relevant scheme was vitiated (see para.74 of the judgment of the Supreme Court in *Reilly and Wilson*). This is an issue of continuing importance as it affects not only the Employment, Skills and Enterprise Scheme but also current schemes under s.17A. The Upper Tribunal's decision and the previous litigation are discussed in detail in the General Note at the beginning of the Jobseekers (Back to Work Schemes) Act.

The right to reside test continues to be a fertile source of court and Upper Tribunal decisions. This year has seen yet more important decisions, which include the CJEU decisions in *Dano v Jobcenter Leipzig* and *Singh v Minister for Justice and Equality*, the Court of Appeal's decision in *Sannah v Secretary of State for Work and Pensions* and the Upper Tribunal's decision in *TG v SSWP (PC)*. These decisions and their implications are analysed in detail, as are all aspects of this complex test, including in particular the further restrictions on the right to reside of EEA jobseekers that have been introduced since the last edition of this volume.

Besides these highlighted developments, there has also been the usual crop of more minor legislative changes and the continuing flow of Upper Tribunal decisions on various aspects of the means-tested benefits covered by this volume. This includes, for instance, a number of decisions on a range of issues concerning the treatment of capital and also housing costs.

As always, revising and updating the legislative text and commentary has required considerable flexibility on the part of the publisher and a great deal of help from a number of sources, including CPAG as advisory editor to the series, for which we express our sincere appreciation. Thanks are also due to Peter Banks, Maggie Phelps, John Bourne and Martin Williams.

To maximise space for explanatory commentary we have provided lists of definitions only where the commentary to the provision is substantial, or where reference to definitions is essential for its proper understanding. Users of this book should always check whether particular words or phrases they are called on to apply have a particular meaning ascribed to them in the legislation. Generally, the first or second regulation in each set of regulations contains definitions of key terms (check the "Arrangement of Regulations" at the beginning of each major set of regulations for an indication of the subject matter covered by each regulation). There are also definition or "interpretation" sections in each of the Acts (check "Sections Reproduced" at the beginning of each Act for an indication of the subject matter covered by each section or Schedule).

Users of this series, and its predecessors, have over the years provided valuable comments which have invariably been helpful to us in ensuring that the selection of legislative material for inclusion and the commentary upon it reflect the sort of difficulties encountered in practice. In so doing, readers have thus helped shape the content of each of the volumes in this series. We hope that readers will continue that tradition. Please write to the General Editor of this series, Nick Wikeley, c/o School of Law, University of Southampton, Highfield, Southampton SO17 1BJ, who will pass on any comments received to the appropriate commentator.

Our gratitude also goes to the President of the First-tier Tribunal (Social Entitlement Chamber) and his staff for continuing the tradition of help and encouragement.

July 2015

Penny Wood
Richard Poynter
Nick Wikeley
John Mesher

CONTENTS

PART I
BENEFITS ACTS

PART II
INCOME SUPPORT

Contents

Contents

PART III
OLD STYLE JOBSEEKER'S ALLOWANCE

Contents

PART IV
STATE PENSION CREDIT

PART V
THE SOCIAL FUND

PART VI
NEW STYLE JOBSEEKER'S ALLOWANCE

USING THIS BOOK: AN INTRODUCTION TO
LEGISLATION AND CASE LAW

Introduction

This book is not a general introduction to, or general textbook on, the law relating to social security but it is nonetheless concerned with both of the principal sources of social security law—*legislation* (both primary and secondary) and *case law*. It sets out the text of the most important legislation, as currently in force, and then there is added commentary that refers to the relevant case law. Lawyers will be familiar with this style of publication, which inevitably follows the structure of the legislation.

This note is designed primarily to assist readers who are not lawyers to find their way around the legislation and to understand the references to case law, but information it contains about how to find social security case law is intended to be of assistance to lawyers too.

Primary legislation

Primary legislation of the United Kingdom Parliament consists of *Acts of Parliament* (also known as *statutes*). They will have been introduced to Parliament as *Bills*. There are opportunities for Members of Parliament and peers to debate individual clauses and to vote on amendments before a Bill is passed and becomes an Act (at which point the clauses become sections). No tribunal or court has the power to disapply, or hold to be invalid, an Act of Parliament unless it is inconsistent with European Union law.

An Act is known by its "short title", which incorporates the year in which it was passed (e.g. the Social Security Contributions and Benefits Act 1992), and is given a chapter number (abbreviated as, for instance, "c.4" indicating that the Act was the fourth passed in that year). It is seldom necessary to refer to the chapter number but it appears in the running heads in this book.

Each *section* (abbreviated as "s." or, in the plural, "ss.") of an Act is numbered and may be divided into *subsections* (abbreviated as "subs." and represented by a number in brackets), which in turn may be divided into *paragraphs* (abbreviated as "para." and represented by a lower case letter in brackets) and *subparagraphs* (abbreviated as "subpara." and represented by a small roman numeral in brackets). Subparagraph (ii) of para.(a) of subs.(1) of s.72 will usually be referred to simply as "s.72(1)(a)(ii)". Upper case letters may be used where additional sections or subsections are inserted by amendment and additional lower case letters may be used where new paragraphs and subparagraphs are inserted. This accounts for the rather ungainly s.171ZS of the Social Security Contributions and Benefits Act 1992 (in Vol.IV).

Sections of a large Act may be grouped into a numbered *Part*, which may even be divided into *Chapters*. It is not usual to refer to a Part or a Chapter unless referring to the whole Part or Chapter.

Where a section would otherwise become unwieldy because it is necessary the Strasbourg case law and are required to interpret domestic legislation, so far as it is possible to do so, to give effect to the incorporated Convention rights. Any court or tribunal may declare secondary legislation incompatible with those rights and, in certain circumstances, invalidate it. Only the higher courts can declare a provision of primary legislation to be incompatible with those rights, but no court, tribunal or Upper Tribunal can invalidate primary legislation. The work of the Strasbourg Court and the impact of the Human Rights Act 1998 on social security are discussed in the commentary in Part IV of *Vol III: Administration, Appeals and the European Dimension.*

See the note to s.3(2) of the Tribunals, Courts and Enforcement Act 2007 in Part V of *Vol III: Administration, Appeals and the European Dimension* for a more detailed and technical consideration of the rules of precedent.

Other sources of information and commentary on social security law

For a comprehensive overview of the social security system in Great Britain, CPAG's *Welfare Benefits and Tax Credits Handbook*, published annually each spring, is unrivalled as a practical introduction from the claimant's viewpoint.

From a different perspective, the Department for Work and Pensions publishes the 14-volume *Decision Makers' Guide* at *https://www.gov.uk/government/collections/decision-makers-guide-staff-guide* and the new *Advice for Decision Making*, which covers personal independence payment, universal credit and the "new" versions of Jobseeker's Allowance and Employment and Support Allowance, at *https://www.gov.uk/government/publications/advice-for-decision-making-staff-guide.* Similarly, Her Majesty's Revenue and Customs publish manuals relating to tax credits, child benefit and guardian's allowance, which they administer, see *http://www.hmrc.gov.uk/thelibrary/manuals-a-z.htm.* (Note that the *Child Benefit Technical Manual* also covers guardian's allowance). These guides and manuals are extremely useful but their interpretation of the law is not binding on tribunals and the courts, being merely internal guidance for the use of decision-makers.

There are a number of other sources of valuable information or commentary on social security case law: see in particular publications such as the *Journal of Social Security Law*, CPAG's *Welfare Rights Bulletin*, *Legal Action* and the *Adviser*. As far as online resources go there is little to beat *Rightsnet* (*http://www.rightsnet.org.uk*). This site contains a wealth of resources for people working in the welfare benefits field but of special relevance in this context are the Commissioners/Upper Tribunal Decisions section of the "Toolkit" area and also the "Briefcase" area which contains summaries of the decisions (with links to the full decisions). Sweet and Maxwell's online subscription service *Westlaw* is another valuable source (*http://www.westlaw.co.uk*), as is the Merrill Corporation's *Casetrack* (*http://www.casetrack.com/ct/casetrack.nsf/index?openframeset*) and LexisNexis *Lexis* (*http://www.lexis.com*).

Conclusion

The Internet provides a vast resource but a search needs to be focused. Social security schemes are essentially statutory and so in Great Britain the legislation which is set out in this series forms the basic structure of social security law. However, the case law shows how the legislation should be interpreted and applied. The commentary in this series should point the way to the case law relevant to each provision and the Internet can then be used to find it where that is necessary.

TABLE OF CASES

Table of Cases

Table of Cases

EHRC	European Human Rights Commission
E.H.R.R.	European Human Rights Reports
EL	employers' liability
E.L.R	Education Law Reports
EMA	Education Maintenance Allowance
EMP	Examining Medical Practitioner
Employment and Support Allowance Regulations	Employment and Support Allowance Regulations 2008
EPS	extended period of sickness
Eq. L.R.	Equality Law Reports
ERA	evoked response audiometry
ERA scheme	Employment, Retention and Advancement scheme
ES	Employment Service
ESA	Employment and Support Allowance
ESA Regs 2013	Employment and Support Allowance Regulations 2013
ESA Regulations	Employment and Support Allowance Regulations 2008
ESA WCAt	Employment and Support Allowance Work Capability Assessment
ESE Scheme	Employment, Skills and Enterprise Scheme
ESE Regulations	Jobseeker's Allowance (Employment, Skills and Enterprise Scheme) Regulations 2011
ESES Regulations	Jobseeker's Allowance (Employment, Skills and Enterprise Scheme) Regulations 2011
ETA 1973	Employment and Training Act 1973
ETA(NI) 1950	Employment and Training Act (Northern Ireland) 1950
ETS	European Treaty Series
EU	European Union
Eu.L.R.	European Law Reports
EWCA Civ	Civil Division of the Court of Appeal (England and Wales)
EWHC Admin	Administrative Court Division of the High Court (England and Wales)
FA 1993	Finance Act 1993
FA 1996	Finance Act 1996
FA 2004	Finance Act 2004
Fam. Law	Family Law
FAS	Financial Assistance Scheme
F.C.R.	Family Court Reporter
FIS	Family Income Supplement
FISMA 2000	Financial Services and Markets Act 2000
F.L.R.	Family Law Reports
FME	further medical evidence

F(No.2)A 2005	Finance (No.2) Act 2005
FOTRA	Free of Tax to Residents Abroad
FRAA	flat rate accrual amount
FSCS	Financial Services Compensation Scheme
FTT	First-tier Tribunal
General Benefit Regulations 1982	Social Security (General Benefit) Regulations 1982
General Regulations	Statutory Shared Parental Pay (General) Regulations 2014
GMP	Guaranteed Minimum Pension
GNVQ	General National Vocational Qualification
GP	General Practitioner
GRA	Gender Recognition Act 2004
GRB	Graduated Retirement Benefit
GRP	Graduated Retirement Pension
HB	Housing Benefit
HBRB	Housing Benefit Review Board
HCD	House of Commons Debates
HCP	healthcare professional
HCV	Hepatitis C virus
Health Service Act	National Health Service Act 2006
Health Service (Wales) Act	National Health Service (Wales) Act 2006
HIV	Human Immunodeficiency Virus
HL	House of Lords
H.L.R.	Housing Law Reports
HMIT	Her Majesty's Inspector of Taxes
HMRC	Her Majesty's Revenue and Customs
HMSO	Her Majesty's Stationery Office
Hospital In-Patients Regulations 1975	Social Security (Hospital In-Patients) Regulations 1975
HP	Health Professional
HPP	Higher Pensioner Premium
HRA 1998	Human Rights Act 1998
H.R.L.R.	Human Rights Law Reports
HRP	Home Responsibilities Protection
HSE	Health and Safety Executive
IAC	Immigration and Asylum Chamber
IAP	Intensive Activity Period
IB	Incapacity Benefit
IB PCA	Incapacity Benefit Personal Capability Assessment
IB Regs	Social Security (Incapacity Benefit) Regulations 1994
IB Regulations	Social Security (Incapacity Benefit) Regulations 1994

Table of Abbreviations used in this Series

IB/IS/SDA	Incapacity Benefits Regime
IBJSA	Income-Based Jobseeker's Allowance
IBS	Irritable Bowel Syndrome
ICA	Invalid Care Allowance
I.C.R.	Industrial Cases Reports
ICTA 1988	Income and Corporation Taxes Act 1988
IFW Regulations	Incapacity for Work (General) Regulations 1995
IH	Inner House of the Court of Session
I.I.	Industrial Injuries
IIAC	Industrial Injuries Advisory Council
IIDB	Industrial Injuries Disablement Benefit
ILO	International Labour Organization
Imm. A.R.	Immigration Appeal Reports
Incapacity for Work Regulations	Social Security (Incapacity for Work) (General) Regulations 1995
Income Support General Regulations	Income Support (General) Regulations 1987
IND	Immigration and Nationality Directorate of the Home Office
I.N.L.R.	Immigration and Nationality Law Reports
I.O.	Insurance Officer
IPPR	Institute of Public Policy Research
IRESA	Income-Related Employment and Support Allowance
I.R.L.R.	Industrial Relations Law Reports
IS	Income Support
IS Regs	Income Support Regulations
IS Regulations	Income Support (General) Regulations 1987
ISA	Individual Savings Account
ISBN	International Standard Book Number
ITA 2007	Income Tax Act 2007
ITEPA 2003	Income Tax, Earnings and Pensions Act 2003
I.T.L. Rep.	International Tax Law Reports
I.T.R.	Industrial Tribunals Reports
ITS	Independent Tribunal Service
ITTOIA 2005	Income Tax (Trading and Other Income) Act 2005
IVB	Invalidity Benefit
IW (General) Regs	Social Security (Incapacity for Work) (General) Regulations 1995
IW (Transitional) Regs	Incapacity for Work (Transitional) Regulations
Jobseeker's Allowance Regulations	Jobseeker's Allowance Regulations 1996
Jobseeker's Regulations 1996	Jobseeker's Allowance Regulations 1996
JSA	Jobseeker's Allowance
JSA 1995	Jobseekers Act 1995

JSA (NI) Regulations	Jobseeker's Allowance (Northern Ireland) Regulations 1996
JSA (Transitional) Regulations	Jobseeker's Allowance (Transitional) Regulations 1996
JSA Regs 1996	Jobseeker's Allowance Regulations 1996
JSA Regs 2013	Jobseeker's Allowance Regulations 2013
JS(NI)O 1995	Jobseekers (Northern Ireland) Order 1995
J.S.S.L.	Journal of Social Security Law
J.S.W.L.	Journal of Social Welfare Law
K.B.	Law Reports, King's Bench
L.& T.R.	Landlord and Tenant Reports
LCW	limited capability for work
LCWA	Limited Capability for Work Assessment
LCWRA	limited capability for work and work-related activity
LEA	local education authority
LEL	Lower Earnings Limit
LET	low earnings threshold
L.G. Rev.	Local Government Review
L.G.L.R.	Local Government Reports
L.J.R.	Law Journal Reports
LRP	liable relative payment
L.S.G.	Law Society Gazette
Luxembourg Court	Court of Justice of the European Union (also referred to as CJEC and ECJ)
MA	Maternity Allowance
MAF	Medical Assessment Framework
Maternity Allowance Regulations	Social Security (Maternity Allowance) Regulations 1987
ME	myalgic encephalomyelitis
Medical Evidence Regulations	Social Security (Medical Evidence) Regulations 1976
MEN	Mandatory Employment Notification
Mesher and Wood	*Income Support, the Social Fund and Family Credit: the Legislation* (1996)
M.H.L.R.	Mental Health Law Reports
MHP	mental health problems
MIG	minimum income guarantee
Migration Regulations	Employment and Support Allowance (Transitional Provisions, Housing Benefit and Council Tax Benefit (Existing Awards) (No.2) Regulations 2010
MP	Member of Parliament
MRSA	methicillin-resistant Staphylococcus aureus
MS	Medical Services
MWA Regulations	Jobseeker's Allowance (Mandatory Work Activity Scheme) Regulations 2011

Table of Abbreviations used in this Series

MWAS Regulations	Jobseeker's Allowance (Mandatory Work Activity Scheme) Regulations 2011
NCB	National Coal Board
NDPD	Notes on the Diagnosis of Prescribed Diseases
NHS	National Health Service
NI	National Insurance
N.I..	Northern Ireland Law Reports
NICA	Northern Ireland Court of Appeal
NICom	Northern Ireland Commissioner
NICs	National Insurance Contributions
NINO	National Insurance Number
NIRS 2	National Insurance Recording System
N.L.J.	New Law Journal
NMC	Nursing and Midwifery Council
Northern Ireland Contributions and Benefits Act	Social Security Contributions and Benefits (Northern Ireland) Act 1992
N.P.C.	New Property Cases
NTC Manual	Clerical procedures manual on tax credits
NUM	National Union of Mineworkers
NUS	National Union of Students
Ogus, Barendt and Wikeley	A. Ogus, E. Barendt and N. Wikeley, *The Law of Social Security* (1995)
Old Cases Act	Industrial Injuries and Diseases (Old Cases) Act 1975
OPB	One Parent Benefit
O.P.L.R.	Occupational Pensions Law Reports
OPSSAT	Office of the President of Social Security Appeal Tribunals
Overlapping Benefits Regulations	Social Security (Overlapping Benefits) Regulations 1975
P	retirement pension case
P. & C.R.	Property and Compensation Reports
para.	paragraph
Pay Regulations	Statutory Paternity Pay and Statutory Adoption Pay (General) Regulations 2002; Statutory Shared Parental Pay (General) Regulations 2014
PAYE	Pay As You Earn
PC	Privy Council
PCA	Personal Capability Assessment
PD	Practice Direction; prescribed disease
Pens. L.R.	Pensions Law Reports
Pensions Act	Pension Schemes Act 1993
PEP	Personal Equity Plan
Persons Abroad Regulations	Social Security Benefit (Persons Abroad) Regulations 1975

Persons Residing Together Regulations	Social Security Benefit (Persons Residing Together) Regulations 1977
PIE	Period of Interruption of Employment
PILON	pay in lieu of notice
PIP	Personal Independence Payment
P.I.Q.R.	Personal Injuries and Quantum Reports
Polygamous Marriages Regulations	Social Security and Family Allowances (Polygamous Marriages) Regulations 1975
PPF	Pension Protection Fund
Prescribed Diseases Regulations	Social Security (Industrial Injuries) (Prescribed Diseases) Regulations 1985
PSCS	Pension Service Computer System
Pt	Part
PTA	pure tone audiometry
P.T.S.R.	Public and Third Sector Law Reports
PTWR 2000	Part-time Workers (Prevention of Less Favourable Treatment) Regulations 2000
PVS	private and voluntary sectors
Q.B.	Queen's Bench Law Reports
QBD	Queen's Bench Division
QEF	qualifying earnings factor
QYP	qualifying young person
r.	rule
R	Reported Decision
R.C.	Rules of the Court of Session
REA	Reduced Earnings Allowance
reg.	regulation
RIPA	Regulation of Investigatory Powers Act 2000
RMO	Responsible Medical Officer
rr.	rules
RR	reference rate
RSI	repetitive strain injury
R.V.R.	Rating & Valuation Reporter
s.	section
S	Scottish Decision
SAP	Statutory Adoption Pay
SAPOE Regulations	Jobseeker's Allowance (Schemes for Assisting Persons to Obtain Employment) Regulations 2013
SAWS	Seasonal Agricultural Work Scheme
SAYE	Save As You Earn
SB	Supplementary Benefit
SBAT	Supplementary Benefit Appeal Tribunal
SBC	Supplementary Benefits Commission
S.C.	Session Cases

S.C. (H.L.)	Session Cases (House of Lords)
S.C. (P.C.)	Session Cases (Privy Council)
S.C.C.R.	Scottish Criminal Case Reports
S.C.L.R.	Scottish Civil Law Reports
Sch.	Schedule
SDA	Severe Disablement Allowance
SDP	Severe Disability Premium
SEC	Social Entitlement Chamber
SEN	special educational needs
SERPS	State Earnings Related Pension Scheme
ShPP	statutory shared parental pay
ShPP Regulations	Statutory Shared Parental Pay (General) Regulations 2014
SI	Statutory Instrument
SIP	Share Incentive Plan
S.J.	Solicitors Journal
S.J.L.B.	Solicitors Journal Law Brief
S.L.T.	Scots Law Times
SMP	Statutory Maternity Pay
SMP (General) Regulations 1986	Statutory Maternity Pay (General) Regulations 1986
SPC	State Pension Credit
SPC Regulations	State Pension Credit Regulations 2002
SPCA 2002	State Pension Credit Act 2002
SPL Regulations	Shared Parental Leave Regulations 2014
SPP	Statutory Paternity Pay
ss.	sections
SS (No.2) A 1980	Social Security (No.2) Act 1980
SSA 1975	Social Security Act 1975
SSA 1977	Social Security Act 1977
SSA 1978	Social Security Act 1978
SSA 1979	Social Security Act 1979
SSA 1981	Social Security Act 1981
SSA 1986	Social Security Act 1986
SSA 1988	Social Security Act 1988
SSA 1989	Social Security Act 1989
SSA 1990	Social Security Act 1990
SSA 1998	Social Security Act 1998
SSAA 1992	Social Security Administration Act 1992
SSAC	Social Security Advisory Committee
SSAT	Social Security Appeals Tribunal
SSCBA 1992	Social Security Contributions and Benefits Act 1992

SSCB(NI)A 1992	Social Security Contributions and Benefits (Northern Ireland) Act 1992
SSCPA 1992	Social Security (Consequential Provisions) Act 1992
SSD	Secretary of State for Defence
SSHBA 1982	Social Security and Housing Benefits Act 1982
SSHD	Secretary of State for the Home Department
SSI	Scottish Statutory Instrument
SS(MP)A 1977	Social Security (Miscellaneous Provisions) Act 1977
SSP	Statutory Sick Pay
SSP (General) Regulations	Statutory Sick Pay (General) Regulations 1982
SSPA 1975	Social Security Pensions Act 1975
SSPP	statutory shared parental pay
SSWP	Secretary of State for Work and Pensions
State Pension Credit Regulations	State Pension Credit Regulations 2002
S.T.C.	Simon's Tax Cases
S.T.C. (S.C.D.)	Simon's Tax Cases: Special Commissioners' Decisions
S.T.I.	Simon's Tax Intelligence
STIB	Short-Term Incapacity Benefit
subpara.	subparagraph
subs.	subsection
T	Tribunal of Commissioners' Decision
T.C.	Tax Cases
TCA 1999	Tax Credits Act 1999
TCA 2002	Tax Credits Act 2002
TCC	Technology and Construction Court
TCEA 2007	Tribunals, Courts and Enforcement Act 2007
TCGA 1992	Taxation of Chargeable Gains Act 2002
TCTM	*Tax Credits Technical Manual*
TEC	Treaty Establishing the European Community
TEU	Treaty on European Union
TFEU	Treaty on the Functioning of the European Union
TIOPA 2010	Taxation (International and Other Provisions) Act 2010
TMA 1970	Taxes Management Act 1970
T.R.	Taxation Reports
Transfer of Functions Act	Social Security Contributions (Transfer of Functions etc.) Act 1999
Tribunal Procedure Rules	...Tribunal Procedure (First-tier Tribunal) (Social Entitlement Chamber) Rules 2008
UB	Unemployment Benefit
UC	Universal Credit

UC Regs 2013	Universal Credit Regulations 2013
UC Regulations	Universal Credit Regulations 2013
UCITS	Undertakings for Collective Investments in Transferable Securities
UKAIT	UK Asylum and Immigration Tribunal
UKBA	UK Border Agency of the Home Office
UKCC	United Kingdom Central Council for Nursing, Midwifery and Health Visiting
UKFTT	United Kingdom First-tier Tribunal Tax Chamber
UKHL	United Kingdom House of Lords
U.K.H.R.R.	United Kingdom Human Rights Reports
UKSC	United Kingdom Supreme Court
UKUT	United Kingdom Upper Tribunal
UN	United Nations
URL	uniform resource locator
USI Regs	Social Security (Unemployment, Sickness and Invalidity Benefit) Regulations 1983
USI Regulations	Social Security (Unemployment, Sickness and Invalidity Benefit) Regulations 1983
UT	Upper Tribunal
VAT	Value Added Tax
VCM	vinyl chloride monomer
Vol.	Volume
VWF	Vibration White Finger
W	Welsh Decision
WCA	Work Capability Assessment
WCAt	limited capability for work assessment
WFHRAt	Work-Focused Health-Related Assessment
WFI	work-focused interview
WFTC	Working Families Tax Credit
Wikeley, Annotations	N. Wikeley, "Annotations to Jobseekers Act 1995 (c.18)" in *Current Law Statutes Annotated* (1995)
Wikeley, Ogus and Barendt	Wikeley, Ogus and Barendt, *The Law of Social Security* (2002)
W.L.R.	Weekly Law Reports
Workmen's Compensation Acts	Workmen's Compensation Acts 1925 to 1945
WP	Widow's Pension
WPS	War Pensions Scheme
WRA 2007	Welfare Reform Act 2007
WRA 2009	Welfare Reform Act 2009
WRA 2012	Welfare Reform Act 2012
W-RA Regulations	Employment and Support Allowance (Work-Related Activity) Regulations 2011
WRAAt	Work-Related Activity Assessment

WRPA 1999	Welfare Reform and Pensions Act 1999
WRP(NI)O 1999	Welfare Reform and Pensions (Northern Ireland) Order 1999
WTC	Working Tax Credit
WTC Regulations	Working Tax Credit (Entitlement and Maximum Rate) Regulations 2002

PART I

BENEFITS ACTS

Social Security Contributions and Benefits Act 1992

(1992 C.4)

PART VII

INCOME-RELATED BENEFITS

General

Income-related benefits

1.2   **123.**—(1) Prescribed schemes shall provide for the following benefits (in this Act referred to as "income-related benefits")—

(a) income support;
(b) [⁴. . .];
(c) [⁴. . .];
(d) housing benefit; and
[¹(e) council tax benefit.]

(2) The Secretary of State shall make copies of schemes prescribed under subsection (1)(a), (b) or (c) above available for public inspection at local offices of [³ the Department of Work and Pensions] at all reasonable hours without payment.

[Subss. (3)–(4) omitted as applying only to housing benefit and council tax benefit.]

AMENDMENTS

1. Local Government Finance Act 1992 Sch.9 para.1(1) (April 1, 1993).
2. Tax Credits Act 1999 Sch.1 paras 1 and 2(f) (October 5, 1999).
3. Secretaries of State for Education and Skills and for Work and Pensions Order 2002 (SI 2002/1397) art.12 and Sch. para.9 (June 27, 2002).
4. Tax Credits Act 2002 s.60 and Sch.6 (April 8, 2003).

Income support

124.—(1) A person in Great Britain is entitled to income support if—   1.3
[¹(a) he is of or over the age of 16;]
[⁴(aa) he has not attained the qualifying age for state pension credit;]
  (b) he has no income or his income does not exceed the applicable amount;
  (c) he is not engaged in remunerative work and, if he is a member of a [⁶ couple], the other member is not so engaged; [¹. . .]
[¹(d) except in such circumstances as may be prescribed, he is not receiving relevant education;
  (e) he falls within a prescribed category of person; [⁵ . . .]
  (f) he is not entitled to a jobseeker's allowance and, if he is a member of a [⁶ couple], the other member of the couple is not [³, and the couple are not,] entitled to an income-based jobseeker's allowance.] [⁴ [⁹. . .]
  (g) if he is a member of a [⁶ couple], the other member of the couple is not entitled to state pension credit.] [⁸ ; and
  (h) he is not entitled to an employment and support allowance and, if he is a member of a couple, the other member of the couple is not entitled to an income-related employment and support allowance.]
[¹⁰(1A) Regulations under paragraph (e) of subsection (1) must secure that a person who-
  (a) is not a member of a couple, and
  (b) is responsible for, and a member of the same household as, a child under the age of 5,
falls within a category of person prescribed under that paragraph.]
  (2) [². . .].
  (3) [². . .].
  (4) Subject to subsection (5) below, where a person is entitled to income support, then—
  (a) if he has no income, the amount shall be the applicable amount; and
  (b) if he has income, the amount shall be the difference between his income and the applicable amount.
  (5) Where a person is entitled to income support for a period to which this subsection applies, the amount payable for that period shall be calculated in such manner as may be prescribed.
  (6) Subsection (5) above applies—
  (a) to a period of less than a week which is the whole period for which income support is payable; and
  (b) to any other period of less than a week for which it is payable.
[⁸ (7) In this section, "income-related employment and support allowance" means an income-related allowance under Part 1 of the Welfare Reform Act 2007 (employment and support allowance).]

AMENDMENTS

  1. Jobseekers Act 1995 Sch.2 para.30 (October 7, 1996).
  2. Jobseekers Act 1995 Sch.3 (October 7, 1996).
  3. Welfare Reform and Pensions Act 1999 Sch.8 para.28 (March 19, 2001).

4. State Pension Credit Act 2002 s.14 and Sch.2 paras 1 and 2 (October 6, 2003).

5. State Pension Credit Act 2002 s.21 and Sch.3 (October 6, 2003).

6. Civil Partnership Act 2004 s.254(1) Sch.24 para.42 (December 5, 2005).

7. Welfare Reform Act 2007 s.28 and Sch.3 para.9 (October 27, 2008).

8. Welfare Reform Act 2007 s.28 and Sch.3 para.10 (October 27, 2008).

9. Welfare Reform Act 2007 s.67 and Sch.8 (October 27, 2008).

10. Welfare Reform Act 2009 s.3(1) (May 21, 2012). (Note that s.3(1) had been amended before it came into force. Section 58(1) and (2) of the Welfare Reform Act 2012, brought into force on March 20, 2012 by art.2(1)(c) of the Welfare Reform Act 2012 (Commencement No. 1) Order 2012 (SI 2012/863) replaced "7" with "5" in the new subs.(1A)(b)).

DEFINITIONS

"Great Britain"—see s.172(a).
"income-based jobseeker's allowance"—see s.137(1) and Jobseekers Act s.35(1).
"couple"—see s.137(1).
"prescribed"—*ibid.*
"qualifying age for state pension credit"—*ibid.*

GENERAL NOTE

Subsection (1)

1.4   Here the general conditions of entitlement to income support are set out. Note the amendments made on October 7, 1996, on October 6, 2003, and on October 27, 2009 as a consequence of the introduction of, respectively, jobseeker's allowance ("JSA"), state pension credit ("SPC") and employment and support allowance ("ESA") (see below). All of the conditions must be satisfied for there to be entitlement to income support (*CIS 166/1994*). There is also a capital test under s.134(1).

If there is entitlement under this subsection, the amount of income support is laid down in subss.(4)–(6).

There is no contributions test or requirement of citizenship (but see s.115 of the Immigration and Asylum Act 1999 on "persons subject to immigration control"). However, although a person qualifies if he is in Great Britain, an habitual residence condition was introduced on August 1, 1994 and a right to reside condition on May 1, 2004. See the definition of "person from abroad" in reg.21AA of the Income Support (General) Regulations and the notes to that definition. Regulation 4 of the Income Support Regulations allows an award to continue for a short period of temporary absence from Great Britain, but otherwise income support cannot be paid to a person outside Great Britain. See *R(IS) 4/99* and *R(IS) 9/98*, which hold that income support is not a social security benefit within art.4(1) of EC reg.1408/71. Although income support has been listed by the UK Government as included in the new category of "special non-contributory benefits" to which reg.1408/71 applies from June 1, 1992 (see art.4(2a) and Annex IIa), such benefits cannot be "exported" (i.e. paid where the claimant is in another Member State) (art.10a). Article 10a provides for the granting of such benefits "exclusively in the territory of the Member State in which [the person] reside[s], in accordance with the legislation of that State". ("Resides" means "habitually resides": art.1(h).) It was argued in *Perry v Chief Adjudication Officer, The Times*, October 20, 1998, also reported as part of *R(IS) 4/99*, that art.10a conferred a positive right to income support on the claimant because of his habitual residence in the UK, and that he remained entitled to income support by virtue of that right, even during periods of temporary absence. However, the Court of Appeal rejected this argument. The language of art.10a made it clear that special non-contributory benefits were to be granted in accordance with the domestic law of the Member State. Presence in Great Britain was a requirement of the UK's legislation (subject to the exceptions in reg.4 of the Income Support Regulations) and this was not incompatible with art.10a. The Court of Appeal also agreed with the Commissioner that the claimant could not rely on art.2(4) of EC Regulation 1247/92 (the Regulation which introduced the June 1992 amendment) to export an entitlement to income support in respect of periods before June 1, 1992.

Paragraph (a)

From October 7, 1996 the minimum age for income support is again 16 (as it was until September 1988 before most 16- and 17-year-olds were excluded). But to be entitled a person must fall within a prescribed category (para.(e)). See reg.4ZA of and Sch.1B to the Income Support Regulations for these categories. Note that a person aged 16 to 18 in relevant education is still only entitled to income support in certain circumstances (para.(d) and reg.13 of the Income Support Regulations).

1.5

The reduction in the lower age limit is a consequence of the replacement from October 7, 1996 of income support by income-based JSA for people who are required to be available for work as a condition of receiving benefit. To be entitled to income-based JSA a person must in general be at least 18 (Jobseekers Act s.3(1)(f)(i)), although there are exceptions, which are similar, but not identical, to those that used to operate for income support (see the 1996 edition of J. Mesher and P. Wood, *Income Support, the Social Fund and Family Credit: the Legislation* for reg.13A of and Sch.1A to the Income Support Regulations and the further escape under s.25; these provisions were revoked on October 7, 1996). Entitlement to JSA, SPC or ESA excludes entitlement to income support (paras (f)–(h)).

Paragraph (aa)

State Pension Credit was introduced on October 6, 2003. Paragraph (aa) rules out any possibility that a claimant could be entitled to both state pension credit and income support by providing that no person who has reached "the qualifying age for state pension credit" can be entitled to income support. "The qualifying age for state pension credit" is defined by s.137(1) below. The effect of that definition is that the qualifying age was 60 for both men and women until April 2010 and will now increase by stages to 65 in line with the increase in pensionable age for a woman. It remains possible for the partner of a person over 60 to claim income support in some circumstances—see para.(g) below.

1.6

Paragraph (b)

The person's income (which includes the income of the claimant's family) must be less than the applicable amount (effectively the figure set for the family's require-ments under s.135). However, note that as a consequence of the removal of amounts for children from income support (with effect from April 6, 2004, except in "tran-sitional cases"—see the note to reg.17 of the Income Support Regulations), only a partner's income will count as that of the claimant and the applicable amount will no longer include any personal allowances for children, the family premium, the disabled child premium or an enhanced disability premium for a child.

1.7

CIS 166/1994 confirms that the conditions in subs.(1) are cumulative. The fact that the claimant was not working in his business and so para.(c) did not apply, did not mean that income from that business could not potentially disentitle him under para.(b). See the notes to reg.30 of the Income Support Regulations.

Paragraph (c)

The introduction of the condition in para.(c) marked an important change from the supplementary benefit rules. If either the claimant or his partner is in remu-nerative work (defined in regs 5 and 6 of the Income Support Regulations) there is no entitlement to income support. For supplementary benefit, this condition was only applied to the claimant. The transitional protection announced on April 28, 1988 (see p.198 of the 1998 edition of *Mesher and Wood*) has remained on an extra-statutory basis.

1.8

Note that from October 7, 1996 the limit for remunerative work in the case of a partner is 24 hours or more a week (Income Support Regulations reg.5(1A)). It remains 16 or more for the claimant.

Paragraph (d)

1.9   See regs 12 and 13 of the Income Support Regulations.

Paragraph (e)

1.10   From October 7, 1996 only certain categories of people are entitled to income support. See reg.4ZA of and Sch.1B to the Income Support Regulations for these categories. They are similar to those groups who formerly were exempt from the requirement to be available for work for the purposes of income support (see Sch.1 to the Income Support Regulations which was revoked on October 7, 1996), but there are some differences.

Paragraph (f)

1.11   Entitlement to JSA excludes entitlement to income support (any "top-up" to a person's contribution-based JSA will be by way of income-based JSA, not income support); if the claimant is a member of a couple, he will also not qualify for income support if his partner is entitled to income-based JSA or if he and his partner are entitled together to "joint-claim" JSA. But although entitlement to income support and JSA is mutually exclusive, some people may be eligible for either, i.e. those who fall into a prescribed category for income support but who also satisfy the labour market conditions for JSA. See the notes to reg.4ZA of the Income Support Regulations for discussion of the position of such claimants and of the fact that the raising of the limit for remunerative work for partners to 24 hours a week from October 7, 1996 may create a "better-off" problem for some claimants.

Paragraph (g)

1.12   By virtue of para.(aa) above, a claimant who has reached the qualifying age for state pension credit cannot be entitled to income support. Claimants who have not themselves reached the qualifying age for state pension credit, but who have partners above that age, may claim income support as long as their partners are not actually entitled to state pension credit. Since, under s.1 SSAA 1992, there can be no entitlement to state pension credit without making a claim, the effect is that couples with one member who has reached the qualifying age for state pension credit and one member who has not (and who are not already in receipt of state pension credit) can choose to claim either income support, JSA, or ESA (according to the circumstances of the member who has not reached pensionable age), or state pension credit. It will normally be advantageous to claim state pension credit.

Paragraph (h)

1.13   Entitlement to ESA excludes entitlement to IS (as does a partner's entitlement to income-related (but not contribution-related) ESA). See the note on the Introduction of ESA in the commentary to para.7 of Sch.1B (below).

Subsection (1A)

1.14   See para.1 of Sch.IB to the Income Support Regulations and the notes to that paragraph.

Subsection (4)

1.15   This provision sets out the basic means test calculation for income support. Providing that the conditions of entitlement imposed by subs.(1) and the capital test under s.134(1) are satisfied, the claimant's income is set against his applicable amount, calculated according to regs 17–22 of the Income Support (General) Regulations. The difference is the amount of benefit. The claimant's income includes that of the other members of his family, except in prescribed cases (s.136(1)). Note that as a consequence of the removal of amounts for children from income support (with effect from April 6, 2004, except in "transitional cases"—see further the note to reg.17 of the Income Support Regulations), only a partner's income will count as that of the claimant.

Subsections (5) and (6)
These provisions allow regulations to deal with entitlement for part-weeks. See regs 73–77 of the Income Support (General) Regulations.

1.16

Severe hardship cases

125.—[¹. . .]

1.17

AMENDMENT

1. Jobseekers Act 1995 Sch.3 (October 7, 1996).

Trade disputes

126.—(1) This section applies to a person, other than a child or a person of a prescribed description—

1.18

(a) who [² is prevented from being entitled to a jobseeker's allowance by section 14 of the Jobseekers Act 1995 (trade disputes)]; or

(b) who would be so [² prevented] if otherwise entitled to that benefit, except during any period shown by the person to be a period of incapacity for work [¹ . . .] or to be within the maternity period.

(2) In subsection (1) above "the maternity period" means the period commencing at the beginning of the 6th week before the expected week of confinement and ending at the end of the 7th week after the week in which confinement takes place.

(3) For the purposes of calculating income support—

(a) so long as this section applies to a person who is not a member of a family, the applicable amount shall be disregarded;

(b) so long as it applies to a person who is a member of a family but is not a member of a [⁴ couple], the portion of the applicable amount which is included in respect of him shall be disregarded;

(c) so long as it applies to one of the members of a [⁴ couple]—

(i) if the applicable amount consists only of an amount in respect of them, it shall be reduced to one half; and

(ii) if it includes other amounts, the portion of it which is included in respect of them shall be reduced to one-half and any further portion of it which is included in respect of the member of the couple to whom this section applies shall be disregarded;

(d) so long as it applies to both members of a [⁴ couple]—

(i) if neither of them is responsible for a child or person of a prescribed description who is a member of the same household, the applicable amount shall be disregarded; and

(ii) in any other case, the portion of the applicable amount which is included in respect of them and any further portion of it which is included in respect of either of them shall be disregarded.

(4) Where a reduction under subsection (3)(c) above would not produce a sum which is a multiple of 5p, the reduction shall be to the nearest lower sum which is such a multiple.

(5) Where this section applies to a person for any period, then, except so far as regulations provide otherwise—

    (a) in calculating the entitlement to income support of that person or a member of his family the following shall be treated as his income and shall not be disregarded—

        (i) any payment which he or a member of his family receives or is entitled to obtain by reason of the person to whom this section applies being without employment for that period; and

        (ii) without prejudice to the generality of sub-paragraph (i) above, any amount which becomes or would on an application duly made, become available to him in that period by way of repayment of income tax deducted from his [³ taxable earnings (as defined by section 10 of the Income Tax (Earnings and Pensions) Act 2003 under PAYE regulations]; and

    (b) any payment by way of income support for that period or any part of it which apart from this paragraph would be made to him, or to a person whose applicable amount is aggregated with his—

        (i) shall not be made if the weekly rate of payment is equal to or less than the relevant sum; or

        (ii) if it is more than the relevant sum, shall be at a weekly rate equal to the difference.

(6) In respect of any period less than a week, subsection (5) above shall have effect subject to such modifications as may be prescribed.

(7) Subject to subsection (8) below, the "relevant sum" for the purposes of subsection (5) above shall be [⁵£40.50].

(8) If an order under section 150 of the Administration Act (annual up-rating) has the effect of increasing payments of income support, from the time when the order comes into force there shall be substituted, in subsection (5)(b) above, for the references to the sum for the time being mentioned in it references to a sum arrived at by—

    (a) increasing that sum by the percentage by which the personal allowance under paragraph 1(1) of Part I of Schedule 2 to the Income Support (General) Regulations 1987 for a single person aged not less than 25 has been increased by the order; and

    (b) if the sum so increased is not a multiple of 50p, disregarding the remainder if it is 25p and, if it is not, rounding it up or down to the nearest 50p,

and the order shall state the substituted sum.

AMENDMENTS

    1. Social Security (Incapacity for Work) Act 1994 Sch.1 para.31 (April 13, 1995).

    2. Jobseekers Act 1995 Sch.2 para.31 (October 7, 1996).

    3. Income Tax (Earnings and Pensions) Act 2003 Sch.6 Pt 2 para.179 (April 6, 2003).

    4. Civil Partnership Act 2004 s.254 and Sch.24 para.43 (December 5, 2005).

    5. Social Security Benefits Up-rating Order 2015 (SI 2015/457) art.16 (April 6, 2015).

DERIVATION

Social Security Act 1986 s.23.

DEFINITIONS

"child"—see s.137(1).
"couple"—*ibid.*

"family"—*ibid.*
"prescribed"—*ibid.*
"the Administration Act"—see s.174.

GENERAL NOTE

The trade dispute rule, long an important part of the supplementary benefit **1.19**
scheme, was considerably simplified in the income support rules, although most of
the stringency remains.

Subsection (1)
The rule applies to anyone other than a child or qualifying young person **1.20**
(Income Support Regulations reg.14) who is disentitled to JSA, or would be disentitled, under s.14 of the Jobseekers Act. Thus the income support rule depends
directly on the JSA rule. Note that if the decision-maker considers that he does
not have enough information to decide this question, it will be assumed that the
person is involved in the trade dispute (Decisions and Appeals Regulations 1999
reg.13(2)).
The rule does not apply when the person involved is incapable of work. The rule
also does not apply in the maternity period, defined in subs.(2).
If the rule applies there are consequences for the way in which applicable amounts
are calculated. This is dealt with in subs.(3). There are also consequences for the
way in which income is calculated. This is dealt with in subs.(5) and in a number
of regulations. The most immediate effect is that the person is treated as in remunerative work for the seven days following the first day of the stoppage of work or
the day on which the claimant withdrew his labour (Income Support Regulations
reg.5(4)). The result is that neither the person nor his partner can be entitled to
income support at all for those days (s.124(1)(c)).

Subsection (3)
This provision sets out the effect on the applicable amount if the claimant is not **1.21**
excluded by the conditions of entitlement.

(a) A single claimant with no child or qualifying young person in the household
is to have no applicable amount, and so cannot be entitled to any benefit.

(b) For a single claimant with a child or qualifying young person in the household, the "portion of the applicable amount included in respect of" the claimant is disregarded. It is clear that the personal allowance for the claimant is
taken out, and so is any premium payable on account of the claimant's disability or age or because she is a carer. Arguably the family premium and the
lone parent element of the family premium (if payable) are not included "in
respect of" the claimant and so remain, but the *Decision Makers Guide* only
accepts this in the case of the basic family premium (see para.32639). But
this point ceased to be relevant when the basic family premium and the family
premium for lone parents became payable at the same rate.

(c) For a couple where the trade dispute rule applies to only one of them, if
they have no premiums on top of their personal allowance, that allowance
is reduced by a half. This is a different rule from supplementary benefit,
which would have left the other partner with the appropriate personal allowance for a single claimant. If there are any premiums, then the rule in para.
(b) applies. Thus any premium payable solely for the person involved in the
dispute (e.g. a carer premium) is taken out, but according to para.32642 of
the *Decision Makers Guide* such a premium will be included in full if it is for
the person not involved in the dispute. Any premium paid for the couple (e.g.
a pensioner premium) is reduced by half. But para.32642 accepts that the
family premium is payable in full. It is easier to argue for the retention of the

family premium here, since that would be paid to the remaining partner if the partner involved in the trade dispute disappeared.

(d) For a couple where the trade dispute rule applies to both of them, the applicable amount is nil if there is no child or qualifying young person in the house-hold. If there is a child or qualifying young person, then the family premium and any premium paid for that person's disability is allowed on top of the personal allowance for that person.

Note that housing costs are payable, provided that at least one member of the family (e.g. a child or qualifying young person) is not involved in the dispute. The housing costs are treated as the responsibility of the member or members not involved in the dispute (Income Support Regulations Sch.3 para.2(2)).

Further, note that the above explanation of the provisions in subs.(3) needs to be modified to take into account the removal of amounts for children and qualifying young persons from income support with effect from April 6, 2004, except for "transitional cases". Transitional cases in this context are income support claimants (i) who were in receipt of the child elements (see below) on April 6, 2004 and who have not subsequently been awarded child tax credit, or (ii) whose families included a child or young person on April 6, 2004, who have not been awarded child tax credit and who made a new claim for income support after that date but before September 8, 2005. Such claimants will continue to receive the child elements, that is, personal allowances, the family premium and premiums for their children as part of their income support until they apply for or are transferred onto child tax credit. This transfer was intended to start in October 2004 but was repeatedly delayed and it now seems the the transfer process will not take place at all and the situation will eventually be resolved by the abolition of income support and child tax credit and their replacement by universal credit. See further the note to reg.17 of the Income Support Regulations.

Subsection (5)

1.22   If the trade dispute rule applies, the normal rules about income are modified. Under para.(a) any payment that a member of the family receives, or is entitled to obtain by reason of the person involved in the trade dispute being without employment, must be taken into account. In *R(SB) 29/85* a loan from a local authority Social Work Department (the Scottish equivalent of a Social Services Department) to meet arrears of hire purchase repayments was held to be capable of being such a payment. The claimant had not been in arrears before the dispute and the loan was to be repaid on his return to work. However, on the facts it was a payment of capital, not income. Although reg.41(3) of the Income Support Regulations (now only still in force in "transitional cases"—see further the note to reg.41(3)) secures that, in trade dispute cases, payments under ss.17, 23B, 23C or 24A of the Children Act 1989 or s.12 of the Social Work (Scotland) Act 1968 or s.29 or s.30 of the Children (Scotland) Act 1995 (payments to families to prevent children being taken into care, etc.) are to be treated as income, not capital. Nor does the disregard of such income in para.28 of Sch.9 to the Income Support Regulations apply in trade dispute cases. Other categories of income normally disregarded but counted here are income in kind (para.21) and charitable, voluntary or personal injury payments (para.15). Holiday pay paid more than four weeks after the termination of employment (normally capital) is earnings (reg.35(1)(d)).

The other main category under para.(a) is income tax refunds paid or due. The effect of reg.48(2) is that in trade dispute cases refunds do not count as capital. The assumption is then that they count as income, but this does not seem to be provided for expressly.

Under para.(b) there is the final automatic deduction of the "relevant sum." This is the sum specified in subs.(6). as increased in future years under subs.(7). The sum was increased to £40.50 in April 2015. The relevant sum is often called